YOU CAN DO IT!

Games

Kirk Bizley

Heinemann
LIBRARY

To Amber

First published in Great Britain by Heinemann Library
Halley Court, Jordan Hill, Oxford OX2 8EJ
a division of Reed Educational and Professional Publishing Ltd.
Heinemann is a registered trademark of Reed Educational & Professional Publishing Limited.

OXFORD MELBOURNE AUCKLAND IBADAN JOHANNESBURG
BLANTYRE GABORONE PORTSMOUTH (NH) USA CHICAGO

Designed by Ken Vail Graphic Design, Cambridge
Illustrations by Graham-Cameron Illustration (Tony O'Donnell)
Originated by Ambassador Litho Ltd
Printed by Wing King Tong in Hong Kong

03 02 01 00 99
10 9 8 7 6 5 4 3 2 1

J 796

ISBN 0 431 08536 6

1246768

British Library Cataloguing in Publication Data

Bizley, Kirk
Games. – (You can do it)
1. Games – Juvenile literature   2. Exercise – Juvenile literature
I. Title
790.1

Acknowledgements
The author would like to thank the staff and pupils of Shepton Mallett Community Infants School.

The Publishers would like to thank the following for permission to reproduce photographs:
Allsport, page 15 (top) / Gary M Prior; Trevor Clifford, pages 4 (top), 5, 11, 12, 16; Empics, page 15
(bottom), 20 /Aubrey Washington, 21; Newitts, page 4 (bottom).

Cover photograph reproduced with permission of Trevor Clifford

Our thanks to Betty Root for her comments in the preparation of this book.

Every effort has been made to contact copyright holders of any material reproduced in this book.
Any omissions will be rectified in subsequent printings if notice is given to the Publisher.

For more information about Heinemann Library books, or to order, please phone 01865 888066,
or send a fax to 01865 314091. You can visit our web site at www.heinemann.co.uk

Contents

Words in bold letters **like these** are explained in the Glossary.

What do you need?

For different games you need different kinds of equipment. The kind of clothing you need is very much the same.

For rounders you need some open space. You also need some posts, rounders bats and a light ball. You can also get a **hitting T** to rest the ball on.

To play short tennis, you need a bat with a short handle, and a ball. To play a game, you need a court which is marked out and has a net.

backboard

ring

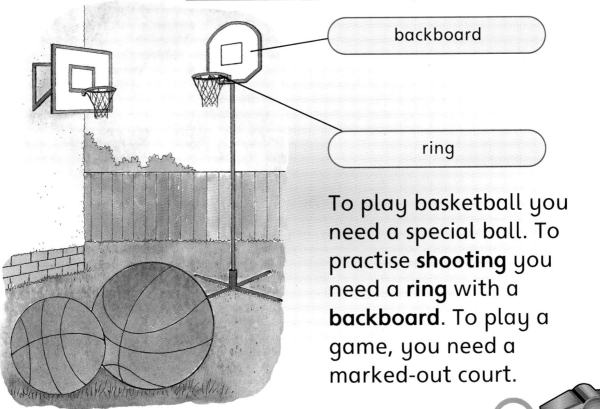

To play basketball you need a special ball. To practise **shooting** you need a **ring** with a **backboard**. To play a game, you need a marked-out court.

Are you ready?

Before you practise or play any game, make sure your body is ready. This is called a **warm-up**. It helps you to play better. It also helps to make sure you don't hurt yourself.

To start with, run around your playing area, or just run on the spot.

Now you need to get your **muscles** warmed-up. The best way is to move your **joints** – your shoulders, elbows, knees and waist.

Try some **stretching** exercises too. These make your muscles warmer and more stretchy so they can move as much as possible.

hamstring and lower back stretch

arm and shoulder stretch

calf stretch

lower back stretch

Rounders

To play rounders you need to be able to throw, catch and hit.

There are two ways of throwing the ball. For a short throw use an **underarm throw**. To throw a bit further, use an **overarm throw**.

Practise catching by throwing a ball up in the air, and catching it as it comes down. Watch the ball all the time. Make a cup shape with your hands and reach out towards the ball as it comes to you.

Practise with a friend, too. Start with an underarm throw and stay quite close together. As you get better, go further apart. You can use the overarm throw now.

Practise hitting with a bat and ball.
Throw the ball to each other using the underarm throw. Don't throw the ball too hard!

Playing rounders

Rounders is a game for two teams of six to nine players. One team **bats**. The other team **bowls** and **fields**. Then they swap.

On a rounders pitch there are places for the bowler and the batter to stand. The fielders stand by the posts. They try to catch the ball.

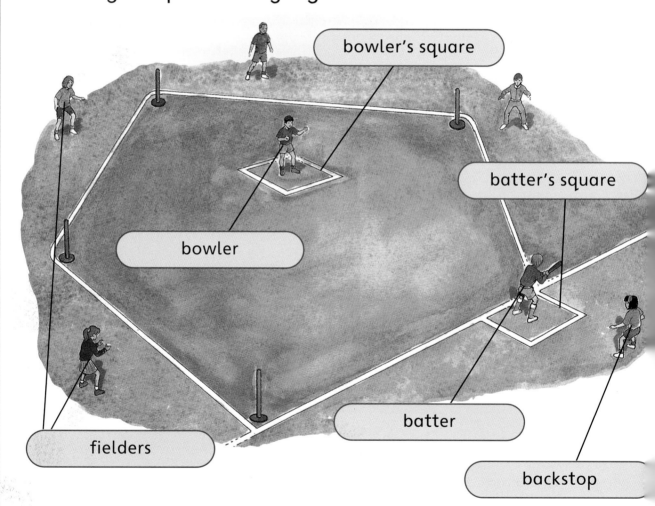

bowler's square

batter's square

bowler

batter

fielders

backstop

The **backstop** stands behind the batter to catch the ball if the batter misses it.

The bowler bowls the ball towards the batter. If the batter hits the ball, they try to run around all of the posts until they get to the last one. If they do this in one go, they score one **rounder**.

The fielders try to catch the ball and throw it to the fielders by the posts.

If a fielder catches the ball before it hits the ground, the batter is out.

If a fielder touches a post with the ball before the batter gets there, the batter is out.

At the end, the team with the most rounders wins!

Short tennis

To play short tennis you need a bat and ball. The bat is like a tennis racket but with a shorter handle and a larger head.

First, get used to your bat and ball. Do this by hitting the ball up in the air. See how many times you can hit it in a row.

Then try playing against a wall. Make sure the wall is flat and smooth. The ball will bounce back for you to hit again.

With a friend you can hit the ball backwards and forwards to each other. Remember, watch the ball very carefully and don't hit it too hard!

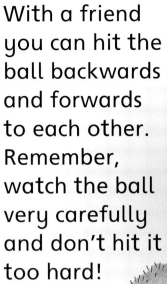

Let the ball bounce just in front of you. Bring your racket back and swing it forward to hit the ball. Watch the ball all the time.

Playing short tennis

This is a short tennis court.

To play you have to be able to hit the ball over the net so it lands inside the lines.

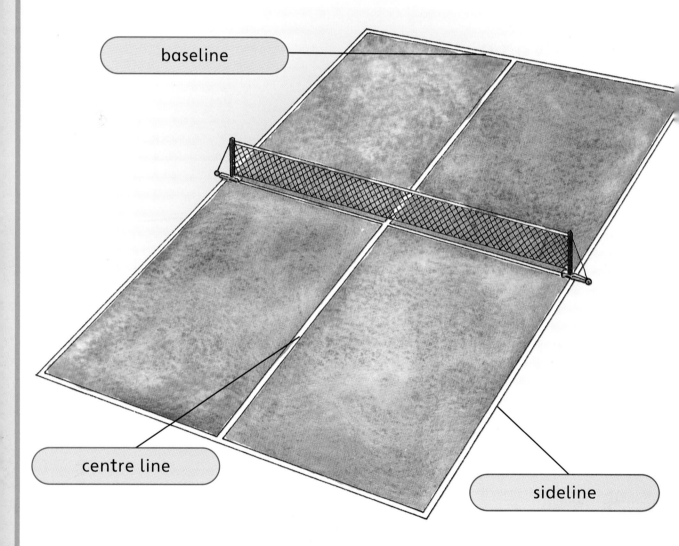

baseline

centre line

sideline

To start a game one player has to **serve**. Stand just outside the court and hit the ball over the net to the other side.

You can play three different kinds of shot. You play **forehand strokes** when the ball comes to the same side of your body that you hold your racket in. It is like hitting the ball with the front of the racket.

You play **backhand strokes** when the ball comes to the other side. It is like hitting the ball with the back of the racket.

A **volley** is when you hit a ball before it has bounced.

Basketball

To play basketball you need the right kind of ball. You can get balls in different sizes. It is better to start with a small one.

Basketballs are bouncy so you can **dribble** with them. Dribbling means bouncing the ball and moving about at the same time. Can you do it?

This is a basketball court. When you play, you have to stay inside the lines.

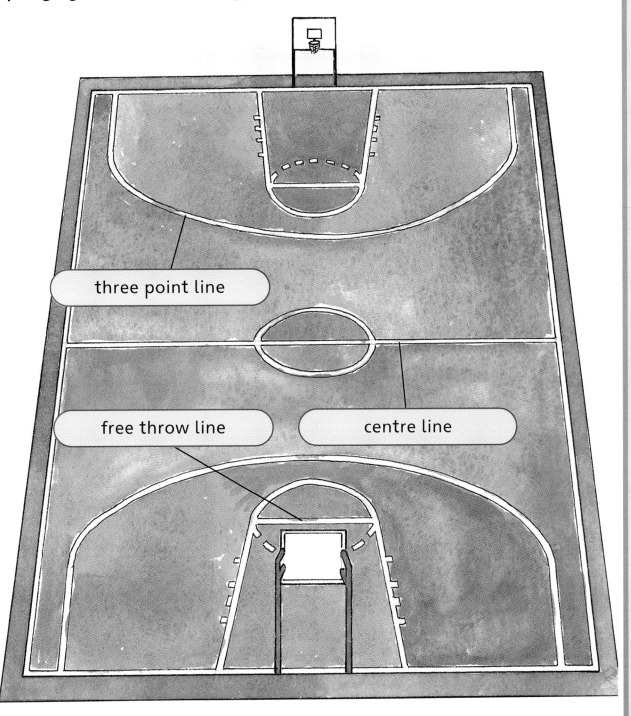

three point line

free throw line

centre line

You score by throwing the ball through the basket. It must go up over the basket and drop down through the net.

Catch and pass

Basketball is played with two teams. Each team has five players. You pass the ball to your team mates, and catch it if they pass to you.

To catch you must watch the ball carefully as it comes towards you.

Move, if you have to, to get behind the ball.

Hold your hands out towards the ball as it gets closer to you.

Catch it with two hands. Bring your arms in towards your body as you catch the ball.

To pass the ball to a player nearby, use a **chest pass**.

Hold the ball by
your chest.
Use both hands
behind the ball.

Push the ball
away from you
and towards a
team mate.

If your team mate
is further away, use
an **overarm pass**.

Hold the ball in one
hand. Lift your arm
up high, with your
elbow straight.
Swing your arm to
throw the ball.

A **bounce pass** is when you make the ball bounce
on the ground before it goes to your team mate.

Dribble and shoot

To **dribble** the ball, you bounce it and move around at the same time. In a proper game you must take more than one step for every bounce of the ball.

Here are some dribbling tips.

Use your fingers, spread out, to push the ball down to the floor.

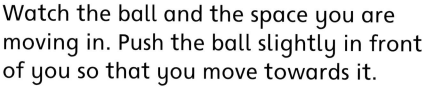

Don't push down too hard or the ball will bounce up too high!

Use both hands so you can change direction easily.

Watch the ball and the space you are moving in. Push the ball slightly in front of you so that you move towards it.

Move slowly at first.

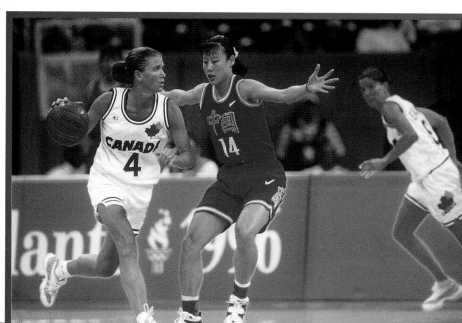

The best way to practise **shooting** is to use a proper basketball **ring** and **backboard**.

Stand quite close to the basket and slightly to the side.

Always aim the ball at the backboard. Then it should bounce back down through the basket. Don't throw too hard!

To shoot from further away you have to throw the ball harder.

Make sure you are behind the ball when you throw. Bend down and then push up as you shoot.

Rules

Different games have different rules. Here are some of the rules for rounders, short tennis and basketball.

Rounders

When you bat, you can be out of the game if a fielder catches the ball you hit before it touches the ground. Or if a fielder hits a post with the ball while you are running between posts. Or even if you drop your bat!

You have to run around all of the posts and touch the last one to score a **rounder**.

You usually only get one chance to hit the ball. But the bowler must throw again if she or he throws a 'no ball'. A no ball happens if it is **bowled** above your head, below your knee, not in reach of you or straight at your body.

Short tennis

You must keep the ball inside the lines all the time.
If it lands on the line, it is in.
The ball is only allowed to bounce once.
The ball has to go over the net.
You have to stand outside the court when you **serve**.

Basketball

You are not allowed to run with the ball.
When you move with the ball you must **dribble** it.
Never touch any of the other players to get the ball.
The ball, and you, must stay inside the court.
If you touch the line you are out of court.

Safety

Don't play games in dangerous places. Never play anywhere near roads.

Have a grown-up in charge of a game so that everyone plays by the rules.

The grown-up in charge should check any equipment you use. If you see anything wrong, tell them!

Equipment should only be moved by grown-ups.

Make sure that you are dressed properly for any game.

You must have a proper **warm-up** to get yourself ready.

Cool-down

When you have finished, you should have a **cool-down**. This is to let your body get back to normal after all the work it has done.

A simple way to cool down is to do all the things you did in your warm-up. Do fewer of the stretches and for less time.

If you do all these things you will enjoy yourself and be safe. Remember,

YOU CAN DO IT!

Glossary

backboard board which holds the shooting ring for basketball

backhand stroke tennis shots played with the back of the racket

backstop fielder who stands behind the batter in rounders

bat hitting the ball in rounders

bounce pass pass where the ball hits the ground first

bowl throwing the ball to the batter

chest pass throwing the ball from chest high in a game of basketball

cool-down exercises to relax your body after a game

dribble/dribbling bouncing the ball and running in basketball

field catching and throwing the ball in rounders

forehand stroke tennis shot played with the front of the racket

hamstring large group of muscles at top, back, of your legs

hitting T stand for the ball to sit on in rounders

joints parts of your body where two bones join together, like your shoulders, elbows and knees

muscles part of your body which help you to bend and stretch

overarm pass throwing the ball with your arm up high

ring circle which the ball must go through to score in basketball

rounder making a score in rounders. At the end of a game, the team with the most rounders wins.

serve way of starting a game of short tennis

shooting trying to throw the ball at the backboard so it drops through the ring in basketball

stretching moving your joints and muscles as much as you can

underarm throw throwing a ball up with your arm starting down low

volley hitting a ball before it hits the ground

warm-up way of moving to get your body ready for exercise

Index